"For maximum benefit, read That Audible Sli[...]
you will hear the whirr of birds, the click of Fa[...]
awake to its own listenings and jostlings within the rivers of
the world. However you read this book, take it in, you will feel yourself hearing anew.
Rest awhile in this consciousness."

—RONNA BLOOM, poet

"Within That Audible Slippage each measure of the text invites a deeper hearing,
in an entrancing dance of sounds vividly musical and politically astute. Twinned
ironic anchors of popular culture and natural silence yield by turns whispers, yells,
and experience."

—SHEILA MURPHY, author of Permission to Relax

That Audible Slippage

UNIVERSITY *of* **ALBERTA** PRESS

That
Audible
Slippage

MARGARET CHRISTAKOS

Published by

University of Alberta Press
1–16 Rutherford Library South
11204 89 Avenue NW
Edmonton, Alberta, Canada   T6G 2J4
amiskwaciwâskahikan | Treaty 6 |
Métis Territory
uap.ualberta.ca | uapress@ualberta.ca

LIBRARY AND ARCHIVES CANADA
CATALOGUING IN PUBLICATION

Title: That audible slippage / Margaret
    Christakos.
Names: Christakos, Margaret, author.
Series: Robert Kroetsch series.
Description: Series statement: Robert Kroetsch
    series | Poems.
Identifiers: Canadiana (print) 20230551793 |
    Canadiana (ebook) 20230551807 |
    ISBN 9781772127393 (softcover) |
    ISBN 9781772127584 (EPUB) |
    ISBN 9781772127591 (PDF)
Subjects: LCGFT: Poetry.
Classification: LCC PS8555.H675 T53 2024 |
    DDC C811/.54—dc23

First edition, first printing, 2024.
First printed and bound in Canada by
Houghton Boston Printers, Saskatoon,
Saskatchewan.
Copyediting by Kimmy Beach.
Proofreading by Mary Lou Roy.

A volume in the Robert Kroetsch Series.

University of Alberta Press is committed to
protecting our natural environment. As part
of our efforts, this book is printed on Enviro
Paper: it contains 100% post-consumer
recycled fibres and is acid- and chlorine-free.

University of Alberta Press gratefully
acknowledges the support received for its
publishing program from the Government of
Canada, the Canada Council for the Arts, and
the Government of Alberta through the Alberta
Media Fund.

To those listening

Actually, if you run into people who are really interested in hearing sounds, you're apt to find them fascinated by the quiet ones.

"Did you hear that?" they will say.

—JOHN CAGE, *Indeterminacy*

Contents

1   1/ A Branch of Happen

2   Capacity

6   Rise Unclutter Path

10   Contest Enter People

13   Collision Altercation Allegedly

15   Branch

19   Paper Crowns

21   Feed the Birds

30   Aluminum Machiavellian Allegations

36   Hours

38   Such Love Alert

42   Chairs Bending at the Hips

43   Upload

45   Station

46   Gloss

49 2/ Heart Is a Guest Whippet Resting on a Firm Trunk

61 3/ Listening Line Notebook

73 4/ The Incubation

91 *Notes & Acknowledgements*

1
A Branch
of Happen

Capacity

Way in or a way back
walking on frozen shore & all

the skate rental stands have only racers

Snow's triage some
mist in the layers of air & others also
              breathing
deep frost exhale that shows itself
repeats blooming

From the front of your face cloud-
swollen balloon of crystal Each head

disappears into its own exhaust
every walker billowed
into the dayscape where ice
has precedence

You need a long time to set
the scene you aren't
awake

Are partially hovering
somewhere in a long frost-
lined aqueduct
afloat on one side
as if flying or swimming

erect like a neighbour's post-box flag

You flutter between these bodily

stations wearing clothes while
glistening naked your shape is
visible & camouflaged

You are only partially
languaged at least half your brain
ribbets & growls sentences
of minced emotion

You hear shirred whooshings
of water in a rush over rock beds

There's no point in indicating any
one object for the location keeps
flopdiving in a backward pivot

There's no fragrance & every
smell nothing smooth or
an entire continuity
Skin unravelling as
velvet to moss

Like they said it's not a
place or a particular body
you are riding but a whinnying rip
in the tendon

Bells whortle Twigs snap
Forest is a strip mall

You cough into the drive-in order box
Black tea with milk two

sugars Young squirrel hands over

a paper sac for all your valuables Sky blue
gown flaps open at the back as

if you're a window

Rise Unclutter Path

So first —

        root out what's

        starting to form in the mist at the field's
        edge those

        tatters of becoming

        *

All the voices being held at bay

       their dull finish

       like the paths in patina left by
       blackboard erasers

       green-felt clogged with chalk

       The board like rock, cold
       or quiet, rubbed

       in the voices you first woke to

       *

At the endgame in the mist of this field's

thick idea

a floating-smoke island

tamped low as juniper's foliage

Its white cloud fog-bombing each brain, pale

lumps sitting
on green stems

ink muffles

*

Clamour like a murmuring flock that could scatter

        into eyesight

        black wings lickchopping air

        bird chatter until

                voices unclutter,   as if

         rehearsing

           to hear

Contest Enter People

      Suction from a snowplow

      Crack of light from the bathroom (one can see the shampoo)

      Furnace aguzzle & drizzle pops
          heated air on the move, sifting upward

      Influxury of the self audible all about
      some blood moon
                  An eclipsing
      mind in which memory spills
      its irremedial sepia slew —

No —

      don't want to be

      awake Want to gather
      in the snow-grey valley
      amidst what can be dreamt of

      To push & draw closer to all who are dead —
      flicking each silver breastbone against the supershine
      of a noteworthy lunar event

Want to gather in the valley
of snow-grey senses

           How you are listening —

CORRUPTION BITUMEN COURT DATE

investigation industry traffic
update the robots are coming

Billionaire says *The humanities matter*

Anyone can enter our contest

Let's stay awake out there people —

Just stir yourself once
in forever under this ultra blown
bleeding moon-thing
          & snap back into day

Collision Altercation Allegedly

Imagine bodies on ledges
mother watches her son shot in the head
corners of dreaming jut into live signal
the hole through ear canals
behind where eyes fill with water

Voices fill at the words
Pull of the corners
jutting from dreams into eyes making them leak
holes of ears
mouth ajar tasting snow's flat
light outside the window

Whose speech warrants coverage
whose uncovered head in news
how many shoes were left
unmoved after the mosque shootings

Loud votive recognition dreams

who is still in all the rooms
jutting into the future
who has been protected by a police review board

While other relative voices
scream *NOOOO* on the radio

Airwaves pulsing with a gaping opportunity to
do more than listen
even if what you mourn

swallows

Branch

Voices you cannot remember so
    recent present &
scattered into the snow dunes
    of what's become passed
over

    Just that audible slippage
so quick so natural
    like the motion of winter birds
adhering to each other in a shared tree
    to fast arcs of solo flight

You're thinking of birds with a muddle
of meanings Birds as voices that leave
              & resettle into snowy retrospect &

birds as the way words are heard
        on the radio
contoured & urgent so
        formed in the ear then how
they vacate so other words

        take their place
How each of the noticed
        transmissions dissipates

into something heard, hard & firm to
        a phrase
no longer crisp or quotable

Now a fuzzed wing of
buzzwords flapping beyond

      listening body into what is
past

Asprint from a rested
      presence of what's up into
the rush & vectored push of up-
      up-&-away & then other birds

arrive & land into ear their small
      clawed feet curling around the listener's
brain stem

      Digging in

for a deepset sonic
      structure of notice

That's it that's

a branch of happen

What happened — More news
at ten for example

Amtrak passenger train collided freight train
South Carolina those not injured being duly
processed

Take note

Memorize

Squeal with the heard misfortune whose
branchwork ballasts

Paper Crowns

Last night at 2:00 a.m. the howling of coyotes at the foot
of 100A Street the
air crystalline with a fierce cold

Was it their echo in river valley wind
this blue morning?

Now, sky fills with large clouds, white froth
loping in from the east, soaked in colonial sludge
   — Vicious words
streaming from white mouths after they acquitted
Stanley and, without a shred of disguise,
white jurors fled out the court's back door
police-protected, cowards panting
for their tiny bomb shelter

Tonight redoubled,
coyotes howl in a circle of darkness
& frigid air vibrates
     The brutally clear current
below river ice firing
refusals into the long night —
Justice for Colten

All day at the university I see many of us, our
paper crowns afloat, distracted guests on this land,
our white ears attuned to the sharp missiles of
settler harm
for how long after?

Feed the Birds

Dream radio clicks on then you
push it off you press into
the box to silence it
                    You crush
within the soft glut sponge guts
of beginning to awaken yet
clinging to dreams as an island
upon which the dead walk near

Maybe that's it   That's as far as
you'll go   you'll allow
the beloved dead their nightly
constitutionals
                    Your dead —
        hover above and the island also
seems like a drone afloat
over the chasm of chance

        Shadows flicker just now indicating
a followable trail

Maybe —
     The house entire starts to
jiggle as if a gear is flung
open —
     There was the open gas
flame, blue, shirring from the hall
vent, amber night lamp overarching
its hot swarm & you leaned
in & clicked the switch off

Lucky there was no fireburst
across the house's third floor
but then again some of the dead
already were & you were protecting
them/yourself —

Merely noticing what is
an open flame & one that still
can be doused

     Watch for what's
on fire

Act in kind even
if you miss that radiant blue
burn & hiss of the process
after

Even when the silence
gloms onto your skull at each ear
& begins to push a channel
violently across the cranial space between

You assume

inland sea would at that point
rush in, unmitigated

That's when people speak of the island's
underground river,
its drive to surge
to storm like a waterfall turned
on its side but without any waning of water volume
displacing across
its tubular hollow

                Just imagine
that going on constantly
behind your nose, below
your eyes   Storm drain
crashing with runoff —
ringed flood-surge
scouring the corridor
into one ear out the other
& so on
               Your head on its own
bobbing in the larger oceanic
cosmos — an island adrift as

a drone, watched from above by a
smaller metallic humanmade
floater-drone, whirring —

That's surveillance

                    Granted
some of the dead seep in sideways
&, again, it looks (or
it would look if you could see it)
like they are swimming
through you, although perhaps there's
a scale issue with the
image   Very small creatures
robust as seahorses on their spine
floating by, making polite
yet rather cursory
conversation

Funerals
        are like that.

Whatever the form —
        what you needed was the guarantee
about seeing them again &
then you were
okay with it

& Then you have to go & take
a rather large   , there's
nothing you can do about it —
it comes *through* you
        something that is made rather
than taken yet you know
it supersedes your creative
control

If it's a poem it recalls
Ginsberg
                one of the dead
who likes to dance by an open-
pit bonfire whose heat
slaps your whole torso

There's no
manual switch   It's
about the time it will require
to be inside the channel
& come through it   The dead
also move urgently
deciding when they need
release

What's clear is the body you are
so proud of holding separate & sealed
only looks that way
from the drone's optimal
pitch

      In fact
you are a morphology of subdermal
rivers of channels
& tubing through which the dead
visit even if it is easier
to imagine the human insides
awash in Gatorade, pesto
& coffee

The house clucks & ticks, its
pipes burbling with the gas-fuelled
heat & in the outdoor pine
a community of chickadees twerps,
whistles
                    There's rarely a silent
second once you turn your attention
to the flow of
discernible presences

The drone
is not picking up on this set
of events even with its fancy
microphonic
scanners   It cannot separate
the dailiness of the dead
from its anxiety
about death   & so nothing is
normal
                    Nothing belongs.

All the rivers moving through their
thought processes probably have
to do with radio &
waking
to its voices — Reporting on the projects
people want to make in the Edmonton
river valley
                  & how Christine
asked you to feed the birds
daily & how none of your beloveds
live out here on the prairies

Yet they flow in you with
ease & with
insistence you

      hear them.

Aluminum Machiavellian Allegations

Hands particularly numb
today holding this pen's
as hard as unscrewing a jar
maybe you should slap a tariff
on lids everywhere Fuck
you lids why won't you
fuck right off & let me
open you

                To punish is to wish you
                suppose

You heard another poet
recently disparage writing
the personal Let's all go
global & historical exhume our
little troubles as if the shuddering
volcanic parachute of the future's
about to rupture Putin
has missiles that can duck &
weave you'll never intercept
Putin's mischief there's no
point chesting your poker
hand any longer Lay
it down says Putin Lay
it out

Hand particularly numb this
morning unscrewing the jam jar's
as hard as deploying your
grip on this pen's scribble
through the probable cosmos of
the bare page firing
off its load of
j'accuse

you allege

you were so incredibly pompous last
night to the cab driver who
took forty-five minutes to arrive he said
he'd been ducking & weaving
through the hockey traffic on ice-covered Jasper
besides calling a taxi with groceries
is a double privilege &
laziness & a
crap shoot
A good back-seat driver shuts
the hell up &
tips high & you

know this but
j'accuse encore

You allege
You have the steel-cased weapons to back
up your cranky evening
You have a button to alloy
every argument you are
the devil so *back off, destiny*

Last night in the observatory
the massive telescopes sat mute
while a graduate student described the thick
cumulus cover overhead
as a domestic impasse

For the evening one had to
believe in the beyond
without visual
evidence

Strangely afterward you meandered
to the atrium in the Forestry
building & sat watching on
your cell a brief video
of a young blind girl who had
received an organ donation of new eyes & was
looking her mother's face
up & down for the first
time — her pupils ducking &
weaving in a skitterish

ecstasy over the cliffs
& galaxies of a face
she'd only known as a key chart of maternal
communicative
elaborations   Her lids now
straining as wide open as they could
Her mouth blinking &
falling empty into a new brand of
belief

O Science what a missile
you make when the goal
is to wish & not

to punish   You allege an
aluminum tenderness
        exists
Some luminous surrender —
A minus time —
A zero gain —
heroic aim at
the straightforward desire for
a firmer grip on some kind of
optimism   Some bargain
with lived lucidity, slick
enough to unlid the
mysteries of the spheres of human devilry
To lay bare our quivering and mutual
presence — *j'accuse j'accuse*
j'accuse

Hours

Your thoughts pitch from topic to topic as the posts
        slide by   You could glom onto one but the cascade
                of new topics persists   Don't be attached   Let the news
                        run through your system   On a bus you review all

                        you now know & discover most of the new fluff
            has fled   So unlike waterbugs hanging in the meadow path
      brushed off like spores of some dream that can't reside
in words once your eyes split open to daylight   Yet

still they imprinted   You were walking together in the meadow
        She showed you bark   leaves   holes banged into moribund trunks
            Berries   You picture each one in a self-quiz this afternoon
              You could retrace the walk   could identify some of

                    those same species now   A million doses of antibiotic arrive
            in Madagascar against the recidivist plague   Bubonic   It's hitting
      the population   She eats a chokecherry   An Eastern European couple has
buckets for their harvest later you both watch them haul

out into their car trunk   They yell they make delicious tea
      She whispers to you, no, wine is the only good use for those
          bright sour capsules pulled from their
              branch-stems   but without alibi you won't taste

              To the whistle of birdseed she calls in the chickadees —
        those little claws dig in & you ditheringly sigh delight
    If only a Twitter link sank into your palm cheek
you'd be better informed   It doesn't rain   No slither

of garters nothing inhospitable nor the least terrifying
      stirs under the deadwood tangle this afternoon   Later
          on the bus you enumerate all the momentous smells in the
              new news under your thumb's manic gobble   You are

              catching up to your vital culture — Say, what did you miss —
    those hours?

Such Love Alert

You either know it or you don't know
what it was supposed to become &
who was slotted to help deliver the basket
of goods to Grandma on the other side of the
forest

You either repeat yourself or go back & read the first part

You check out the past or you plod forward into a mudscape
of original genius

You can tell yourself you're not the *you* but whyever then
do you crave to trim the balcony with heather?

Put us in the deepest weave of the meadow
Let us wander through a labyrinth to make
it back to Grandma's hot bed where her
respirator is on auto

If you didn't check your phone in the last fifteen
you might not get the GLOBAL ALERT the GLOBAL

ALERT Is calling you personally
& you still do not get it

You either know it or you become the basket

You check out the patter of small feet in your foyer
& loop the floral trim loosely enough to leave time
to curl your hair, for the relatives love
to arrive & eat all the stew then ankle
it back to the suburbs

If you *get* the GLOBAL ALERT then go on with the presentation

If you don't get it stumble back to the warehouse
& unsynch your electronics

If you detach your aspirations Grandma
might choke on her voting record for the winner
already declared at two minutes to Armageddon —

or she might be better today than
last month

Honestly you need to access a second opinion on
matters of the present moment without taking
the time to read over what it is you're
just not getting anymore

If you don't get the GLOBAL ALERT climb on up
to someone's penthouse & jam for a while
on their solar keyboards with a cold one
& a moist heat in the sedan's carbon idle

Make it all stretchable so the curviest non-binary
in the borough can slip into something
most comfortable then [*snap*] there goes the fashion
empire

Caping for nightfall to wink at its blue-screen paramour
let's wear our hooded hopes on the runway of the leavy ravine
wondering [*goodness!*] how time asserts itself

At least half of us didn't get the call, still,
we wait like robot panda bears uploading our points
to the recycling schedule & 3D-printing
our own blue bags in the back lane — because

who *knows* where they go?

Take for granted, some persons
on the faster network are already getting this like
pandemic viral strains through the wires

We know we're on the track to a collapsing stadium
with scarlet roses on every railing

It's all *sooooo* decorated   For there's such wild

love [*ha*] in the human impulse to
leave it [*so much!*] better than
we found it

Chairs Bending at the Hips

I'm not sure where or why
our constellations were alike
chairs holding us by the hips
our forearms warmed on
the soft wood
the slick comet stream

                        cool atmosphere circulating freely
                        swaying away an ineffable virus
                        wafting as river will do

My north pole and my south pole
forget how to converse
stymied so that futurity
congeals in the larynx's
uncertainty
though all I know I want
is to sound chorally with you
in the present tensors of spacetime near you
in tuning encounters before hummed flows
erupt from our mouths

                    Are we in a country in a city
                    What is land in the sentient gut
                    How do others navigate at this same juncture
                    via the same chairs
                    conducting us by the hips
                    this multivocal moment
                    this same relative era
                    held to the ear

Upload

A crack from above — the light smashes the fence
You are metres away inside a room trimmed in glass
The light seems lemon for a moment

You can't see the source
All you compute is the fact of the light as it
smacks your face   It smacks the vases around you —

obliterates green   It slaps your nails —
huge hand alighting on your own
Why don't you get up from your chair? No —

You take a picture & post it to Instagram but
the light has learned to uphold itself
Before you get there the photo of the fence

flashes back at you from your feed   It's inside
your sights as if it dreamt your waking this morning
at the moment the mouse's neck was sprung

dead in a trap while in the nightmare you felt

one side of your body burn alive — A nuclear explosion
crept in a tidal whoosh through the room & bodies

vaporized — Yes — it was both immensely fast & very
slow   You liked the art direction Truly
original but woke to the little wisecrack of the mouse's end

saw the lemon light — horizontal — catapult
onto the back gate   There are three more photos
on your feed you don't want to admit

you never took for they've been liked
by dozens   Two different strangers private-message you
How on earth did you get that shot?

Station

Within all of it
you put these hands in the soil
communities stir & name themselves

Within all of this feeling you
dismember grammar
unravel your processions of logic

Against repetition of the same
against the byproduct of failures of imagination
some people will always need to leave

Within your bodies
you hold your intention to be sustained

Hold your slings of hope

Gloss

           audible sound produced by roughened articular
surfaces moving over each other tendons or ligaments
         this *slip* upper over bones whether such changes are
            improvements or evidence of *slipping* standards
slips profound but our *slips* not actual *slips* of the tongue
      are *audible slips* also changes corona discharge levels
    this *audible* noise permit *slipping* off damage failure
       incomplete conductor one of more common ways
this *slippage* occurs alert *audible* signal to advise designated
     persons of fire emergency to ward against tripping *slipping*
       falling drowning collision every fault line
    has upper limit determined by this length width how far
it can *slip* be alert for *audible* air leaks
    around brake components *slipped* lines that electric induction

                    people hips snapping sensation as bands

               ligaments or tendons *slip* this study shows

bad wheel bearing *audible* one easy adjustment

                              no *audible* battery notifications for

               this peaceful sleep true had struggled with earphones

slipping out during early sleep causal crepitation *audible* click during motion

                    didn't seem important at her life's end *slipping* away

          alert *audible* signal to advise designated persons *slippage*

between human performer & demonic character revealing

                    boundary between control detects wheel *slippage* applies brake

                    one of more common ways this *slippage* occurs

per day *audible* speech errors common among younger "click"

          indicates your baby breaking the seal on nipple to *slip*

in baby's mouth *slipping* subluxation of rib cartilage

                              if this main drive chain *slips* off no rows are planting

               "no seed flow" flashes on screen this *audible* alarm

2
Heart Is a Guest Whippet
Resting on a Firm Trunk

1/

the whole body walks through the meadow into the river valley

the spine springs to life allowing the body to slant and descend along the soft
earthen slope

the pelvis sways and notches from one gear to the next, toggling thighs and
knees, causing small blossoms to squeeze and release in the calf muscles

the mouth searches the air like a frond of new asparagus, feels like a slim
tongue as it opens and tastes

the nostrils tingle with moss

the hands

the shoulder blades

the pituitary gland unfurls

the lungs heave and shiver, gush with oxygen, rustle, lust for the gift of gulping in, letting go, of tilting and issuing a stream of exhaust, they allow their system of intake and giving back, giving in to the much larger lung around them

awake

the heart is a guest whippet resting on a firm trunk

individual the body walks into the river valley through the meadowed becoming green

allowing the body to slant and descend the spine springs to life along the soft earthen slope

toggling thighs and knees causing small blossoms of squeeze and release in the calf muscles the pelvis sways and notches from one gear to the next

as it emerges and tastes, the slim tongue searches the air like a frond of new asparagus

with moss the nostrils tingle

hands

bladed shoulders

pituitary unfurls its gland

gush with oxygen they rustle they lust, lungs heave and shiver forth the gift of
gulping in, letting go, of tilting and streaming exhaust

giving in to the much larger lung around them they allow their system
of intake and giving back

awake with eyes closed

on a firm trunk the guest heart is a whippet resting

some go into the river valley on feet with calves and thighs and pelvises

walk among the trees with lungs and pituitary gland and shoulder blades

ears twitch like moths half stuck in a nest made by magpies

ear flippers both inside and outside the thin twig matrix

ear is both inside the body and outside of it like a hinge small and warm

ear makes a sound like crust or crest or a crisscross of breath exhausted by body blossoming back into the larger air

from ear-heard to air-borne

carrying cochlea into the river valley walking by the firm trunks of trees like a guest whippet needs to rest on the soft earthen slope

move slowly so as to hear body awake in this green becoming

4/

don't you know there is colour in the darkness and that the green also
burgeons at night but it doesn't matter for the eyes have sorrow and joy
layered from time to form the smooth lids

                            to keep distance and
deliver light the eyelids move into the river valley carrying us in sorrow
and joy past firm trunks toward the motion of water

                                 the silvered blue its
dark green skin this luminous pelt the shirring current tugging and
suggesting how a body can float awake and sink awake and float

5 /

but it's possible unnerved
in the river valley

         scurrying crows,
         their beak-threaded gaze

picturesque
click within
a fraught place

       abandoned luggage, pink
       scarves, floral prints, menstrual pads

compartments spread-eagled like a pair of huge thighs

        saws; cut trunks,
        branches, upright stumps
        the broken limbs,
        deadfall, dropped
        skinned and blunted

                  muted somehow

a woman's voice on a parallel
path: *i like watching it; i don't
like being in it*

        overturned plinth stamped
        "P R O M I S E S" — performance art surviving
        harsh seasons

                mud-caked backpacks, plaid
                strewn sweatshirts,
                black-furred stuffed animal
                    meshed in soil

past distant trunks figure
walking oversized camo-
pattern
hoisted on his shoulders in
large circles

        garbaged paper
        scraps in leaf cover

                awake, have a camera

6 /

still mark and remark
its local sublime

can't help it
of the visited picturesque of
the iris
even in stillness

taking photographs is —

you make inadequate

they do so
of your forearm

but also breathed air
and light
some inordinate healthfulness

                              and so on

7/

river the valley the float and pituitary

guest joy sorrowing in the lid's furrows

sorrow like joy in the slow blink of the guest whippet resting for a moment

interval of several exhales then

knees pulsing awake on the crooked roots near the firm trunk

throbbing at the back of the walk like a memory of some sorrow

in the lower spine

        in the cushions

           of the lilt on

              the earthen slope

3
Listening Line
Notebook

to self:

           if I watch you draw
           your own listening   does it
           undo time

try
listening with eyes open
                closed
         ears "directed"
            undirected

try
listening + smelling + breathing

to self:

push that nib with your desire

to feel it slip at its own pace

continue listening + sniffing the air

every now + again

open eyes — begin anew on

path

to self:

eyes closed   —   ears open
two selves
two times
eyes open watching hand
          not watching   hand active
                    passive

so many permutations   one alike the other

drawing   making it "something"

               sketching a record

                                        outline of
                                        a mound

                                        a monument

    ears closed   —   ?

                                        can't hear

edge of a cloud

    that torn suitcase

to draw your hand
drawing

eyes fidget

one line listening to

radio interview

~~not watching~~ eyes slip

      left to right
      right to left

      two continuous lines
      eyes glimmer

avert

overt

a

vesicle

particle   air

portal

report

discern

late-breaking appeal

this distance

an overturn

a partition

ambiguous affiliation

a pushback

capitulation

this cold return

brink of

contradictation

visceral flight

a denial

this rapid learning

to hear

to have
            heard

                        verdict

                                    to listen

                                    to have

                        listened

shelter in place

discern contours of others

      one continuous line   two eyes

             ears

             do they open

             do they

               undo

4
The
Incubation

To get my comeuppance — no —
to arrive into the present
to sit under a tree &
the buzzing begins

•

Thirsting for air the brain becomes a mind —
a book of trees — branched
synapses that span the planet —
crowns of laurel sprouting through skull
carried like baskets of raw grain
atop a stick-straight spine

This human category like a gate
of Heaven through which only
the two-leggeds proceed weeping

•

Another mother robin in the poplar nest above —
randy chickadees incessant
in their status updates —
trains cars air conditioners subsumed
in the buzzing of late July crickets
Mueller's testimony disappointing the committees
Boris Johnson showing his ass-
backward victory pals the riddle
of a hidden chamber where they keep
an all-night poker game boiling
like a dirty vat of oil stinking of pounds
into which the "better" humans
are sacrificed on the hour then
eaten with plenty of Doug Ford's
lukewarm buck-a-beer

•

How did mind warp to brutal
brain or brain
drown in uprooted mind-swamp
for this particular
threshold-moment?

•

You don't ask this if you're busy
under a tree watching minuscule
ants gorge on the carcass
of a white squirrel & when you awaken
a small "plane" brings a box
from Amazon to your back patio
with words like poetry by Frank O'Hara
printed on its shipping receipt —
No returns — no second chances —
You bought it we sold it
& here it is at your gate

Open it — this emergency
Open it — this meditation

•

Get your comeuppance Watch
it arrive under this poplar perfect-bound
like a flock of brains gold
& croaking about collusion
at the highest level while safe
injection sites serve coffee
in Styrofoam cups — & I sit
in the second person
bathed in a monarch's orange
flutter surrounded in three directions
by the minds of birds telling their young
to *Go — fly — go now — go*

•

Well — horrified & lost —
I've been bingeing *Mad Men* on my laptop
using Netflix like a communion —
cathedral of good dramatic writing
with characters we can gobble
& incubate — the Dark Lord
obsession of all of us raised godless
with a special appetite for
Daddy's secret coping mechanism —
one ivory face turned to his daughter's
smile the shaded other tying some cleavaged
bitchy broad to a motel bedpost

•

Writers have a double life dreaming
the lucent storm of contradiction
into characters they can't possibly
kill off — no need to wrestle
with the Real Thing

Endless replay is our gift —
I wouldn't have guessed it but
Donald Trump *is* the spawn — the cold
outcome of Donald Draper in
the creased suit immaculately
prepared for his next
corporate takeover campaign —
Ascending hilton.com to Mars
with a few other billionaires
dressed in laurel wreaths
tweeting & untweeting
& tweeting &
untweeting like a God that keeps
forgetting what he created yesterday
sending out Sarah Huckabee Sanders to say
That never happened — next —
But time stops for everyone — Hell is fresh

•

I like to imagine I'm about 35 —
Somehow my children have joined
the adults' banquet —
the present moment defies me —
my wounds mystify my purpose —

•

But I was born in 1962
& have lived a blessed life
& never once driven a spear hot
into another human's breast — not
directly —

I consider writing an act of communion
with human mind in the present moment

Whether the tree is a real thing
or not — Mind beyond the
human
baffles me

•

Still my synapses flare with birdsong
& I think I'm dying until
another pulse of composition hits —
like the next episode Weiner
didn't get to write

He must wake
in a cold sweat night after
night appalled at leaving
Draper on a fucking mountaintop
with nothing better to say than

I'd like to buy the world —

He didn't have the guts
to show Draper
stepping into North Korea
stroking his long red tie & holding hands
with Kim Jong Un for the Associated Press
Corps' tongue-tied gaggle

At least he took care of Betty —
Bets — *Bye Bye Birdie* — killed
her in America's prime — time —
released Sally to her future
Dark-Lord-Daddy complex
which is all the network
really put in the contract
aside from
"end on *om*" — besides
there are other stories
he wants to tell to get
his comeuppance

•

Other confessions —
I was always terribly embarrassed
the few times in church when
communion was offered — All I knew
was I wasn't confirmed — I
didn't rate — I had to find
another way to eat my Jesus

Poetry was it
Poetry is it — the grand replay
of a suppressed scene —
unsayable purpose —
self-addling lie in waiting —
the crown of laurels that sprouts
from my skull — resurrective

Beeping alarm as the delivery truck
reverses with a massive load
of glass bottles for the craft brewery
in the lane — the modest gardener
sweeps the patio next door —
& crickets accelerate — amplify

Their buzzing trill louder than human mind
above
my human brain

Philip Glass had nothing
on these guys — he had just a musical
idea about the audible world

How humans could incubate
something of our own inside
Nature's obvious divinity — sit
& listen to it — thirst for air —
then fashion a response
to an unintelligible question —
proceed weeping

Arrive at the pressing dilemma

that to listen is to suspend
almost all other moral virtue —
to choke — simultaneously
to await voice

This doubleness of writing that allows
listening to compose itself into
language — silent on the page —
silent in the thirsty air

•

An aria —
incipience —
to incubate the Holy — the way Weiner slid
some howling Ginsberg in along with
Lucky Strike

Because — well — he didn't know what else to
do writing from the future
back to countless moments he could've killed
off Don & let someone
else become eternal
the way Yoko Ono is today

Notes & Acknowledgements

Thank you to friends and family whose encouragement has allowed me to sustain writing life these past decades. My love to CCG, SCG and ZCG, as ever.

Thank you to the Department of English and Film Studies at the University of Alberta for a vibrant writing residency in 2017–2018. Thanks especially to Marilyn Dumont for contouring my residency in Edmonton with such lovely creative kinship. Warm thanks to Janice Williamson for a decades-long term of inspiration. And, thank you to Sheila Greckol for hosting me in her home through the fall of 2018, and to my dear poet-friend Sonja Greckol for hinging us together.

Thank you to Christine Stewart for loaning me her Rossdale cottage in the winter and spring of 2018, where sections of this manuscript found their form. In particular, thank you to Christine and Graham for autosetting their clock radio alarm, thereby delivering public voices to my pillowside, alongside birds, river pings and coyotes.

Thanks for the sociality of other new colleagues in Edmonton, including Shelley Bindon, Christie Schultz, Nathalie Kermoal, Donia Mounsef, Dianne Chisholm, Katherine Binhammer, and Christine Wiesenthal, who kindly brought my work into her classroom for in-class visits. My appreciation as well to Shannon Maguire, Larissa Lai, and other writers who organized readings at the University of Calgary, and poetry gatherings among the many poets I have associated so long with U of A, especially the wonderful Doug Barbour.

Warm appreciation to writers at the U of A who participated in the polyvocal and improvisatory sounding sessions I was exploring in the Canopy project, including Matthew James Weigel, Maria Teodora Barbu, and Luciana Erregue-Sacchi.

Thank you to Smaro Kamboureli and University College at the University of Toronto for hosting me as the Barker Fairley Distinguished Visitor in 2018–2019, which enabled work on this manuscript, and helped sustain writing through the pandemic years. One of the grounding pleasures of this past few years has been to learn about and experience Deep Listening, through the guidance of Anne Bourne and her own generous and rich inhabitation of the tuning meditations and experimental sounding practices of Pauline Oliveros.

Many thanks for support and guidance to Michelle Lobkowicz, and to the excellent and caring production team at University of Alberta Press.

| Some of the poems in this collection have been previously published in earlier forms. "Branch" was prepared in a special letterpress edition in fall 2018 by Someone Editions. "Collision Altercation Allegedly" and "Such Love Alert" were published in the *Humber Literary Review*, Fall/Winter 2018–2019. Thank you to the editors.

"Collision Altercation Allegedly" and "Paper Crowns" refer to the January 29, 2018, episode of CBC Radio's *The Current,* which covered the first-year anniversary of the Québec City 2017 mosque shooting, in which it is noted that "the shoes of the men who were killed that day are still in the same place. No one has touched them." Also in this episode, "Jury selection is set to begin in the case of the Saskatchewan farmer charged with second degree murder in the shooting death of an Indigenous man, Colten Boushie."

"Hours" was written after an introduction to Edmonton's Hawrelak Park.

"Chairs Bending at the Hips" makes reference to Pauline Oliveros' multi-vocal tuning meditations and other practices of choral sounding.

"Gloss" is a found text allowing for the random interleafing of both listening and slipping.

"Listening Line Notebook" situates both drawing and hearing as metaphysical acts that can be performed on a balcony at night.

Open it — this emergency / *Open it* — this meditation

The above two lines in "The Incubation" refer to Frank O'Hara's collection *Meditations in an Emergency*, first published by Grove Press in 1957. The collection is referred to in three episodes of Season 2 of *Mad Men*. (Google it.)

The epigraph by John Cage is taken from *Indeterminacy: New Aspect of Form in Instrumental and Electronic Music*, reading by John Cage and music by David Tudor; Folkways, 1959. Reissued by Smithsonian/Folkways, 1992.

The cover image is a digital photowork by the author, originally taken in the "Courante" section of the Toronto Music Garden in 2021. The landscaping of this public garden interprets the six dance movements of Bach's First Suite for Unaccompanied Cello.